Sugar
Work

KATIE MARYA

Alice James Books
Farmington, Maine
www.alicejamesbooks.org

10 9 8 7 6 5 4 3 2 1

Alice James Books are published by Alice James Poetry Cooperative, Inc., an affiliate of the University of Maine at Farmington.

Alice James Books
114 Prescott Street
Farmington, ME 04938
www.alicejamesbooks.org

Names: Marya, Katie, author.
Title: Sugar work / Katie Marya.
Description: Farmington, ME : Alice James Books, [2022]
Identifiers: LCCN 2021055540 (print) | LCCN 2021055541 (ebook)
ISBN 9781948579261 (paperback) | ISBN 9781948579353 (epub)
Subjects: LCGFT: Poetry.
Classification: LCC PS3613.A79245 S84 2022 (print) | LCC PS3613.A79245
(ebook) | DDC 811/.6--dc23/eng/20211123
LC record available at https://lccn.loc.gov/2021055540
LC ebook record available at https://lccn.loc.gov/2021055541

Alice James Books gratefully acknowledges support from individual donors, private foundations, the University of Maine at Farmington, the National Endowment for the Arts, and the Amazon Literary Partnership. Funded in part by a grant from the Maine Arts Commission, an independent state agency supported by the National Endowment for the Arts.

Cover art: "Niagra" by Ann-Marie Manker, 2013

Sugar
Work

CONTENTS

IV.

V.

for my mom

I.

To the extent that self is formed in opposition to the world, the self disappears.

Louise Glück

Sugar Work

The cake edges the counter
royal and layered
orange cream fondant

punctured
or slit with a knife
or peeled off exactly

white sugar circles
like a saint's corona
my mother

ate it dry   days old
pleasure was always hers
for the taking

I abstained   I was afraid
of the cake
the edible sun

that half naked photo
of her   younger and firmer
dripping in the kitchen

I thought there was no safe
amount of sugar   so I pretended
to take none

Daughter of an Atlanta Stripper

My mom on that stage rehearsing
to Madonna's "Material Girl" —
she wears champagne-pink tights,

her legs ethereal, and the light hits
her chest so gold dust surrounds
her face. A mirror unfolds behind her,

making it hard to choose which side
of her to admire. Three women follow
her 8-counts while I eat chicken nuggets.

They move in unison. One trips, laughs—
they start again, hips gliding back and forth,
knees bruised from the moves on all fours.

In the back I snoop through drawers
of sequined lingerie, tubes of glitter
lipstick. Mom catches me, lets me pick
a scrunchy, lets me apply the lightest pink.

Father

Not here
but in the streets,
lost in the animal

life cracking
in the Atlanta sun.

Holy your goneness.
Holy your disappearing feet.

The Crisis Is Not Knowing

Either I was touched   or I wasn't
but I cannot remember my legs
bathing   age five   with my grandfather.
This happened to my father as a kid
he finally confessed. So we fled   after
the psychologist told my mother nothing
really happened   but I was unsafe
and should not be left alone with him. Years
later my father denied this history   said
my mother made it up. He needed
drug money. I don't know what he needed.
Here I am   mostly fine—sometimes time
goes by without thoughts of them. I touch
myself   drink tea by the window   sex
with my husband   a retreat   open books
Dutch baby pancakes.   Still   I do not know
what the tongue does at night   no memory
separate from stories   a bathroom
a man's hands   sandbox toys float   soap.
Who gets   to say   who persists
in my heavy head?   Answer me folded
clothes   answer me   cleared table
            with your single orchid.

Initial Paroxysm

Plenty of times I wanted to leave, but I swallowed it
like a big white vitamin—

     evening. In our small white room, in a green field, I said:
     Now I will tell you the truth. Something's wrong
     and my whole body wants for another man.

Memory of me packing more solid than the items packed:
antique napkins, the blue spoon and blender, the cast-iron skillet,
my nightclothes, which were your nightclothes. Silent,

     you stood until you couldn't stand any
     longer. I was ashamed to watch you cry.

I spoke to evade you. Three carloads, six flights of new stairs,
five blocks down the road. I got myself alone. I bought a big mirror,
unearthed the mold from my new apartment's fridge, bleached,

     pushed the love seat into one corner, then another.
     I felt my own violence—breath by breath I stayed calm
     enough to believe what I pretended to know

about loss. I tried to recount us, I couldn't see
our ten years together. Or I refused to. Or I didn't try.

Childhood

Lake Lanier, GA

When I was a child I knew my brothers: see
our bodies running in the thunderstorm
down to the lake after we ache ourselves
away from dad   after we move into
that old wooden house   tiny and cedar
we all ache   but our mouths open to the rain
no silence   no more of our father's cocaine
he won't be around Mimi says   and I believe her.

In the night he finds us   takes my brother
away to Tybee Island   we stand in the hallway silent
I dream of the thunderstorm day   how did my father
get back inside   brother is twelve   brother goes
to rehab at thirteen   at fifteen   at nineteen
I beat against the sky for him.   I scream.

Meditations on Mother as House

I know nothing of my mother,
nothing of her thighs stretching
outside in a plastic lawn chair

as she sips a can of Sprite through a straw,
nothing of the light hitting her, nothing
of light. Only the cave of her body.

Mother as house, as chair, as swimming pool, mother as coat,
as waterbed, mother as oven left on with potatoes inside, mother
as chimney, as linen closet smells, mother as one thousand stairs,
mother as floor, mother as refrigerator full of an assortment of juices,
mother as bleached sink and disposal, mother as fluffed couch—
inside the cave of our mothers' bodies we strip the walls and take
what's ours—we don't know better, we don't know what not to do.

The outside of the cave is her mouth
and through it I can see the electric

fireplace she switches on whenever
she likes. She can be loaded

with insatiable holes:
You love me right? I'm good at being

a mom, right? I try to answer her
by cleaning house, making pork chops,

being funny, but she keeps asking me
to crawl to the back of her throat.

It was just your body and mine in our house when you stood naked and firm
in the glass shower while I watched through the mirror and curled the hair
you helped me bleach blonde. You said the house of my body could be
anything I wanted as you twisted my ends with chemical, folded the foil
with your thick, tan hands—I was timid and straight, scared of your fake
boobs, your ability to choose what you wanted, scared of what you wanted:
money, a man, a bigger home, no suffering.

First Sex

The first time I had sex was in my bedroom   my mother
at work   me and the boy fraught with an on-and-off-again
love   he was very Christian   I became that too   and
our sex was sad   if only I had been less afraid
of blow jobs   quick inside me no condom   he pulled
out and I cried in my bathroom   I want to hold my teenage
vulva   pink oval opalescent   you should google *variety*
of vulvas   find the diagram   rows of vulvas   their
distinctions the beginning of all our bodies. I don't want
to die without redoing that sex but he's married. Here.
Let's redo it here: we'd watch a video on the clit in my bed
full of dollar store pillows to look like Beyoncé's from
MTV Cribs   neither one of us ready so we'd drive to
Taco Bell in the Las Vegas heat   I'd say pull over   take
off his baseball jersey and blue hat to reveal his sweaty
hairline   he'd try so hard with his fingers like the video
and I'd pull my mother's coconut oil from my backpack
recalling how she winked   said it was good for everything
we'd both go but not at the same time   the seam of my
low-waist jeans creaming between my legs on the way
home would feel holy.

God

the potholder used
to remove

the potatoes
or the sun

no one chooses
the body

they're born
into

II.

Valentine's Day

Do you think love only exists
because death exists?
I do not want to marry you.

But I do want explosions
of white taffeta and a cake
propped up in my mouth

with your hand for a photo.
Skin is a casing and I hook
mine to yours with a needle.

Linen hands inside gloves all
winter, so soft, so dead looking
and dry. Sex me. Let's shut

everyone out of our ceremony,
let's buy red lipstick and draw
on each other while we float.

Nobody is as ridiculous
as everybody. I love the air
snagging your hair. I love

the walls painted around us.
When I feel a little bit trapped,
you bring me a bowl of water.

I drink. I turn the bowl upside
down to make a hat. I stand on it.
And you do all this too, with
the other bowl I've given you.

Marriage

In a FB message, a prophet says to watch
meat in high heat is to see the dead rising.

A rump roast browns in the oven,
fried chicken pops hot confetti

into the air, the glaze of ham, pink
like the inside of a blood orange—

each meat body turning into food
under the aura of onion and garlic.

The ocean makes me feel small;
its rhythmic gray sends me searching

for him—sometimes sex, sometimes
two miners underground, every inch

the same. Even the skin feels like stone.
To watch a thermometer rise, to spoon

warmth in the middle of the night
is not power. We switch the oven on,

wrap the turkey legs in twine,
follow the inches toward our life

together, white plates tick away time—
the knife cutting to the spine.

An 8-Count for Lovers

Let a lover into your poem
and they'll redecorate your home
make you mash potatoes
maybe pay your loans
5 6 7 8   most days I wake up
stretch-dance in my underwear
in front of the big mirror I bought
after I left my husband.
Most days I tell myself:
you're a lover   god hovers
around you.   I touch my toes
lift and bend my arms. Hard
to have a lover in a poem
hard for the lover
I am hard for a lover
with silver hair and shaking chairs
and hands all on my rows.
Most days I say this prayer:
love love please come love me
touch your hands to my grooves
1 2 3 4   let me be a yellow door
5 6 7 8   lover wall land floor

Work

Atlanta, 1995

Mom picks me up from school and we drive there,
where I sit on red velvet with my homework,

read *A Wrinkle in Time* while Mother Time reveals
language in one place is not the same in another.

Everyone has a nickname here. My mother
performs a different definition of herself—

I listen to define terms: books sweetly spread
open on the table steamy coffee on her

nightstand   center stage   her shoulders
the center of my life   protection   her hands

protecting mine   heat the Georgia clay
under our feet $200 the cost   of my soccer gear

pour   the ramen noodles into our nice blue bowls,
our apartment affordable until we can move. Stars

over my mother's face as my hand rests under hers
and we sit on the curb   drinking   milkshakes.

An Open Call to Single Daughters of Single Mothers

Come and bring your mother's bodies: bring her naked body and her clothed body, the body she had in the kitchen and on the couch, her walking out the door body and her wake up body, bring her tight jeans body, her cleaning body, bring the drive you to school body, and the day job body in beige work pants, bring her bathing suit body, her parallel parking body, her laughing body, her popcorn shovel mouth body—

don't forget her brand new nails body and her discipline body—the do your homework body, her packing body, her jealous and honest body, her vacation body, her long dress body when you graduated from high school and college, bring her very own daughter body, the bare breast body in her mirror body, bring her body in the glass shower, her sleeping body, her sick body—leave Atlanta first home fast with your mother's body danger the man danger the stuck, you'll want to peel off her bronzed skin, to hold her, for the rest of your life.

And bring the materials that go with her bodies: the white linen pants, rayon multi- color shirts, green spandex dress, leather jacket, bring all her purses with their hangy purse things, bring each piece of jewelry: the giant costume rings—the one shaped like a dragonfly—and the glitter bangle bracelets, bring the bedazzled baseball hats and the pile of strappy sandals, her body sprays, her cigarettes, the pictures of you she keeps in her wallet, her Day-Timer, *People* magazines, and her cable TV box, the swimming pool she bought and the plastic storage bin full of your grade school stories, grab all her drinks: the Big Gulp Diet Coke, the McDonald's coffee. Her bodies will need a snack—a cheeseburger, a whole chocolate pie. Don't forget her vitamins and orange juice, the grilled fish and asparagus. Don't leave any of her bodies behind, pile everything into your Toyota Corolla, give her travel body a travel pillow and get here as fast as you can.

Woman with Ocean-Dad

When I see you holding 3-year-old me at the beach
        in that FB photo you post every year on my birthday,

the massive tank of your water life creaks
        open, fills my adult house, chops each pier

at the knees, drowns my husband, the sofa
        and clean towels, my favorite mug and spoon.

I float through this annual lucid coma in search
        of your face, but you are water—a typhoon.

I've tried to tile you in like a pool, freeze you, but your limbs
        became swords. Make a boat and name it *father*

so I could live in you, but there were holes and I sank. You
        pushed me to shore to be a legged creature, to join

the ones with eyes and skin like mine, the waiting ones,
        our hands and mouths open to the sky.

Marriage Is a Room Full of Windows

Today I want to be young like some girl
on Instagram   she's on top of a building
her boyfriend taking the photo as if she is
the sky   as if her body will go on forever

with him staring at it   morning
my husband makes coffee   we sit on
the porch sticking out from our 2nd floor
apartment into the sky   there are small plants

I've kept alive   he says *we have time to*
I go inside   edge myself onto the counter
and right before I come I think *and*
the body does not go on forever.

The Quiet Divorce

A human-size rabbit came to the door of the house
        that was just my house   the house I made alone.

He came in and his fur grew the length of the walls
        covered the walls and I fed him white bean stew

that had been cooking for years in a Crock-Pot.
        He dipped his paw into my prettiest blue bowl

licking it over and over again until he began to crack
        and his skin turned into the desert.

The softness of fur became the softness of dust
        and I could not clean it up. I scooped the dust into jars

with my bare hands but the jars evaporated. It was cold—
        I dragged the space heater around by its cord

scooping and evaporating until I evaporated too.
        This visitation happened every day all day

though I completed other tasks—I never ran out
        of toilet paper   the plants stayed alive   my taxes

thank you cards   laundry   read   slept   tried to knit.
　　　　At night a glass of water appeared by my bed

and without my recollection of thirst or of drinking it
　　　　the glass was empty by morning. This is how it was

until one day it wasn't and I cannot remember when
　　　　the rabbit stopped coming. Or how the dust withdrew.

Father Sends Adult Child Recurrent Text Message

I hope we can begin a wonderful relationship.

I want this story to be over:
the one in which the father is gone—
just off somewhere in a distant place
with a name the adult-child knows
how to say but never visits, only sees
in the background of a photograph posted
by one of the father's friends on the internet,
then thinks *when I learn of my father's death*
I will be thousands of miles away from his body;
the adult-child communicates with the father
via text message every couple of months—
sounds have become too unfamiliar to bear.
This is the story where the adult-child counts
the losses and moves on. The other option means
no self, and the adult-child owes something
to the self because it carried the adult-child
far enough away from the ship floating
in the middle of the sea where the father lives
with no anchors. The adult-child imagines the father
frying an egg, rubbing a soapy washcloth around
his shoulders, dressing himself, putting food
away—to be alive for this long the hands must do
other things besides drugs. The adult-child needs
a cocaine-free zone to protect these images.
He's still alive at 58 years, of which 43 were spent

on the upper deck cracking in the eternal
sun—a sort of miracle. This is a story
of exhausting maintenance. The adult-child
sometimes wishes the father would be ash
already so that a peach tree could be planted
and fertilized in his honor and then the adult-child
could prune unruly limbs, press satin blossoms
against the face, take a peach into the mouth—
add, instead of remove, flesh from the body.

I Want You Different

Once, a woman called our house to tell me
       my mama was a bad bad woman,

so on Friday at the club my mother pulled
       that lady down the stairs by her hair.

Sometimes I walk a whole block before realizing
       I've left my keys in the ignition,

the engine still on, exhaust puffing into falling snow.
       Strange how we only get a singular life. I waste

a lot of time trying to reconcile what I want
       my mother to look like with how she's made

herself look. Tan. I want her boobs to be the same
       shape as mine like they used to be.

Her face is tight. I always go back to us
       in her big bed, lazy Sunday, curtains shut,

KFC and HBO, my pale shoulder leaning
       against her thigh before she'd roll over
         and ask for some space.

Duende Aubade

Through the crowd of grinding
bodies, I leave the low-lit room,
reach the glass door smeared with

fingerprints, grab the firm long handle
the width of the door, not skin.
I would put anything inside me. Why

does the word empty live in my chest?
Exiting, I say to you, leaning against
the wall, tapping the drum on your thigh,

away from the circumference of heat,
I say to you *hello* and realize it's not
anything, but rather, anything firm

like your hands now along my spine,
your mouth on the nape of my neck.
You know my face but not my home

and we're asleep in a pallet I made
on the floor. Daybreak. *Don't go yet*,
I say, while placing a small bowl of wet

blueberries next to your elbow leaning
on an edge, this edge, this scene of ecstasy—
months later and I'm still at this table.

III.

Exaltation

This voice of my voices is fragile.

In my sideways bed I record my voice reading a poem and send it to
the man I love.

The women I love are poets and they write about a divided self.

Liminal self.

Orchestra refusal of a hurried life.

I want to dance but the dancers still buzz that old song where a strong
man lifts up a small   woman.

I want the man I love to pick me up with insoluble words.

His mouth a wooden boat on the lake of my childhood.

I mean to say the sounds of his mouth are a boat in my exile.

There is no country for me except the body.
And my mother's body.

I know the presidents kill those of us who feel in certain ways—

I am not afraid of my feelings anymore: butter beans

on which I squeeze lemon juice, crystal

faces, hot risotto, the duration

of an arrow, that orchestra

of play in the face of sorrow,

joy joy joy joy joy sounds—

the circle in the middle of joy a portal and we are radiant.

No division I shout I shout I shout.

I am indivisible.

I am bread on the floor of the church and I crawl to the beggar outside.

I leave the church.

I accept my solitary outlook.

I accept my skin.

I accept my newness.

I kill the presidents.

I do not rush to gold.

I decide not to hate me.

I paint my friends and listen to the sound of their names sounding from their own mouths.

I've been the lover since the dawn of time except for the time I threw a cup at my brother's face.

I still smell the blood on his bare chest as he runs from the house.

He had been angry his whole life, then I was angry, then he was scared.

Turn of terror.

Rust.

I don't think he had been allowed fear.

I have been a lover except for all the times I wanted men to find me at the center of everything.

I go to the lakeside where the mud is red.

I go to the lakeside and slide in.

I go with my brother.

My palms then my mouth to the water.

My body to the bodies of water.

IV.

The Religion I've Made of My Mother

I believe in ghosts and angels and god or a burst
that made me from love. I believe in a city
where no one is hungry with houses made of native grass
and biodegradable long-term material and the color yellow.
I am inside one of these houses, the one my mother makes
as she disappears—she disappears in the making of it,
she's surrendered, she holds desire by its neck.
She eats the cake, the salmon, the ramen, the drunk's
final piece of bread, the glitter dress. Her mouth engulfs
a McDonald's hamburger in the middle of night. She's lean,
round-brush bangs, bleached blonde. Some years I don't see
my mother then she appears, fearless, not afraid of god or distance
or the ground, not afraid of her own going, like I am.
Acrylic nails with that subtle pink so her hands look more soft
than strong. I believe in her hands. I can't imagine a world without her
in it, eating and smoking. The Marlboro burns near a corner of her lips.
I can't believe in a god who relies on wounds to be seen.

My First Period

I loved a boy in Guatemala—I was thirteen
on a mission trip—the pastor's son, and he loved
me back, both of us noticing our distinctions:

his hair like a shined boot, mine like wet sand.
He called me canchita y linda. Our team slept
in the church sanctuary and late in the night I'd meet

him in the foyer to play cards. He said he wanted
to be a man of God, he longed to build a church
with a wife like his mother. I wasn't interested in that.

I just wanted a world that felt unknowable. I asked
the boy to pray for me so he would have to touch me
and when he put his hands on my shoulders, I bled.

Water

I spend these months
in pleasure:
dance
walk around alone
swim my fingers over
my stomach in the tub.
I feel good.
There is no moon
in this bathroom
because there is
no window—
I light a candle
to make the moon.

Why I Look Just Like My Mother

A scar formed
        between her pelvis and belly button after the doctor
                cut her open to get me out

then we left the place I was born to live in the desert—

        dust billowed behind us   and I didn't see my relatives
for twenty years.

I tried to climb my mother adorned with freckles and moles
        but she said I was safer
                on the desert floor   where I would learn to stand
    alone.

I learned to step on cactus thorns and never feel them, shadows drifted
        around us. Now, I pick at my skin,

        my face peeled by the consuming sun.

Home in Las Vegas

Targets, Best Buys, IHOPs and casinos—
everything a primary color except the stucco

cube house squatting on its track, the pride
my single mother paid for by herself, mostly,

which shouldn't matter at this point—just look
at her trying so hard to make a normal life

for us: she stains the cement floor like mud
finger paint, an impromptu weekend project,

she switches on the electric fireplace for the dog
as we leave to pick up Chinese food so we can sit

in her bed and watch HBO, that's what we do
on Sundays. My prepubescent body wrapped

in booty shorts and a Bon Jovi t-shirt curling
next to her. She makes dinner sometimes,

always pork chops and green beans. Every night
is the end of a hard day. Once we had a pigeon

problem, shit covered the patio—watch her sprinkle
Alka-Seltzer everywhere, even on the phallic yucca,

and whisper *those birds will nibble up these chalky*
pellets, fly far away, and blow up. She rearranges

all the wrought-iron furniture, spruces up the beds
on the floor with no box springs, stocks the pantry

with perfectly lined boxes of Cheez-Its, Slim Jims
and vitamin C. And here I am now telling you

about the shape of me beneath her feather
comforter, our luxury, and the pigeon plucking

and blinking at the skyscraper palm tree, how
that whole world she made came and went so fast.

How the Mouth Opens

The Earth's mouth reveals itself
to my toddler brother: a half dead

bullfinch on damp grass. He lifts
the warm body to its twig legs

and it falls. He repeats the lifting. Repeats.
Repeats. Repeats. My father comes out, says

look away

and throws the bird against
a brick wall. What choice

did Sam have but to run,
tilt his ripe head, open

his eyes to the bird's peach belly,
the silent curve of its small beak?

Ode to Divorce

I am in the low feeling now

everything about you, here

where the brain lifts

the never-ending rally—

if it was right to leave.

to answer *yes*, instead

to lie down in itself.

fault loses its edges,

that blurring green

There's an empty room

with large windows

a grief room for a woman

Sometimes in this winter

my back to the glass

and it makes me love

where we have no flaws,

the quickening ping-pong,

I like that I question

Space now for the ground

of my mouth, for my body

After you've suffered,

fault is the table, the court,

landscape. I forgive me.

in my office building,

and well-tended plants—

who leaves a good man.

I sit on the floor,

just to feel the sun.

Love Poem for My Ex-Husband

Every day we spend together ends
in the past: our bucket full of hair,

my favorite spoons, 100 t-shirts, the bed.
You said *of course the days are faster*

now than in the past, the bucket fills
with half of them. I count time left though

we're not sick. You said *the days are faster,*
we have less of them. This math haunts me.

I count the decades left, we're lucky.
Your name is a song, a river—there

are less of them now—I saw you first
with a surfboard on the lawn. Your name

is also a cantaloupe, pronounced *pay-kiss*
and I crawled into you on the lawn with

that surfboard before biting my lips
gently into the cantaloupe, crawling

into a river slow orange sun quiet warm
before biting my lips into your name I float

on for some time, a river slow orange sun
quiet warm toward Atlanta where I float

on your name for some time, seek the control
none of us have in our hometowns. Remember

my panic attacks after William, my childhood
friend, was shot in the parking lot. Panic. Loud.

You always make the bed because I can't
unsee that gun blasting in the parking lot—

I need the control none of us have because
I can't unsee the panic. My mother says I'm

like a bullet needing the control no one has,
but you say *forget the metaphor, no one's only*

what their mother says. You're my tribe,
a river, a goddamn cantaloupe, everything

your mother said and I'll float my lips on you
forever until every day we spend together ends.

Object Lesson

I wish I could see my dad years before

    all the cocaine.

Sometimes   to keep my senses from falling apart   I pretend
        my 14-year-old father ran home to his mother
        with a sack of milagros over his shoulder

    and a hundred lanyards dangling the pictures of saints

around his neck.

        His favorite might have been St. Maximilian,
        who loved Mary, took an innocent man's place
        in Auschwitz, was injected with carbolic acid
        and thrown into a furnace—

the man he saved saw him canonized years later.

    In a dream   there are lights on me   I'm a lounge singer
        no a teacher

no just someone in a dark room.

My father splits the lights and I divide like a cell
until eight of me stand in black tube skirts, our shoulders
back, looking like fully-fledged women—

the dividing continues.

I shout at my father   *Stop!*   *Let's change the ending!*

No, I can't! he yells   so I just stand there

trying to clear my throats

unclenching my multiple fists.

Excerpt from The Gold Club Trial: Mother

I actually walked into the big Gold Room

up there and all them basketball players

were there, and I walked in

and one of them was getting head.

I got in so much trouble for that,

for walking into that room.

And I walked in. And them.

And I walked in and them

in the big Gold Room up there,

and I walked in and I got into

so much trouble, and they were

getting head, them, in that room.

So much trouble, so much, so much.

Excerpt from The Gold Club Trial: Daughter

When I dance, I see my mother's heart pumping

in that gold room, walking in on all those men,

trying to be a diplomat, trying to hold down

some professionalism in the club, walking in

a light prism, walking in a thief, a master woman

in our time of need; when I dance, I move like her,

my rhythm her rhythm, my swag hers—glitter me

up, tonight I'll let a man glide his hand over the twist

of my hips, we are a schism of wants and needs.

When I dance, I see the beads of sweat down

my mother's chest, her smell in my lungs, cigarettes

and Sea Breeze body cream. Her voice, the way

the owner heard a threat and made her leave. The way

I hear a heron—each of us trying to unfurl our heavy wings.

For the Lover and Not for Who the Lover Loves

The lover is standing on "O" Street
in the sun of summer's final day,
scrolling Instagram, trailing plants,
snooping a woman's profile. The man
the lover loves, he loves this woman,
and the lover envies her happy face.

The lover stares at their own face
in the reversed camera, soft in the street—
the lover wonders how to woman.
Shadows curl over the brick and the day.
Shadows curl over strolling tired men
and the lover walks home to the plants.

The woman on Instagram has perfect plants
and posts pictures of her mother's loving face.
The lover wants to write a poem about a man,
not mothers. Bing! Picture-text of a Grecian street.
The lover's mother smiles below a blue day,
the lover longs for their mother who is a woman

on vacation tan and bright, a bright woman
who hardly calls the lover. Home. *Water the plants,*
says the lover to themselves, *scoop the day*
into a small clear vase, hold it, face it, face

the window, your face in the pink and fuzzy street,
count your fingers and toes and the men

you've loved, think of the good man
you left, how it felt like undoing the woman
you are. The lover stops thinking. The street
is wet and dark and the uninvolved plants
go to sleep. The lover touches their face,
fries an egg in the nightness of day.

Morning. The lover walks into the new day,
decides she's a woman because she loves men,
knows this thinking is treacherous. Her face
is a sun, her bangs sweat. Another woman
says *hey I like your shoes* while planting
herself into a pink Toyota Tacoma. The hot street

in the middle of the sky, each woman's face, the day
lifts its heat, the plants breathe and the men
around relax. The lover walks the bare street.

V.

what I want is an unnamed thing

Lorna Dee Cervantes

Self-Portrait as Lined Seahorse, as Coronet, as the Sun

I am the speckled sun
pillaring above me,

     I am a coronet tilted back, dashes of glint
reflect my succulent black eyes, I am the sun

signifying morning beneath the sea.
I make rituals to mark the day:

     a brief pirouette, a renewal
     of vows to my heat.

My rays thicken and tangle
around me—

     I sink to the ocean floor.
Sometimes I change from red to canary yellow

while my tunnel snout searches for food
through teased seagrass. I have soft teeth.

     At dusk, drowsy, I scoop myself
     into my lip-colored anchor.

I am the whelk—I am the sea
which is a blouse for time

and my crystal body knows this,
my spine rings like a sequoia, like a wick

to the surface, to the wet land, to the spillage
and held breath, to the gold grease covering

my language—
I am my language,

to my father inside
my mother's arched back

moving like the tide until his milky
flood packs into her, to their bodies entwined

on shag carpet, to my mother alone
allowing me to grow me.

I am a tree rooted
to the side of a cliff.

I make myself
from within her

like God cantilevered the whole
earth on gravity.

Loud Thundering Bids Her

My mother sleeps in sheets
then wakes up sweaty needing me,

the foreboding gray haze thick
until I switch on the big light

so she can see my face. This kind
of winter becomes monthly, daily

and I do not know how to be
the thing my mother needs.

It is said all mothers inherit
the sorrow of Demeter:

3,000 years of seasonal death
relived and packed into mitosis,

what exhaustion. I have no concept
of eternal suffering except for what

my mother feels in her bones.
I can't imagine the bed without her

in it   nor the desert where she built
our house alone. Oh Eternal Mother

let me let her rest   let me not
call her back   with thunder.

How My Father Made the World Lighter

My father playing drums is a child learning to walk. Arms raised, knees bending with that first weight, bobble head saying   *I am a galaxy, I am a glass vase breaking, I'm goodness—*

in the low red light, he smiles, chin lifts, sweat, his relaxed slouch allowing his hands and feet to boom clat baboomboom clat. My child's view of the addict: his aspirations, his cocaine, his piles of car parts, the bad deals, the stray cats and strange lovers, his parents. A view can be a violence, no matter the vision.

When he dies, I'll walk into a house I don't know, take only his cracking drumsticks, hang them in my hallway, touch them,   say *Oh yes, those were my father's.*

A Response to the 2018 IPCC Report

for KSH and MIH

I look at your daughter and feel
cavernous—big face of time.
I miss my ex-husband and the child
we didn't have. I envy how the heavy
you which is the heavy me
has found a solvent place in your body.
How your daughter's desire to look
and eat and wobble and sing tree
is curative, is balm, the good fat,
the exhaustion of living that turns
us to sleep. Cells divide and make
a human, make skin, make avocado
mushed into her bright nose. A baby
is the acceptance of time. The fear
of time narrowed if the body is able
to focus on the body. I read the report,
too. The one that says the margins will be
the first to go, the mothers and fathers
on land's edge: New Orleans, Haiti,
the small wedge of Georgia where my
brother lives. I wish light had a voice,
a sound. I wish it would say out loud:
I am a lover. Why do we have eyes
if we must close them to see? Please,
light, make a sound. You wrote *let me*

believe the work I do can bring
the future into the room. Whether it
does or not. Whether it does or not.

The Artist, After Time Has Passed

The moon knows I wanted to take everything into my mouth as water,
no matter the oaths. Our separating was quiet. I k/now my body's knowledge.
I know now how the body can and cannot be trusted. I remember the end:

he's unhinging my favorite intaglio print from the kitchen wall—
the one I've kept. How gently he handles the art he made. He's asking,
in the harshest tone I'd heard from him, *So you're just going to try men*

until they taste like you want? I long to hear his other voice, the one
explaining the process: how he covered the copper plate in soft ground,
a protective coating; how he tethered it to a post and placed it in a dry

riverbed; how the wildlife scurried over it; how the water rose and fell,
branches and leaves; how it stayed there for the time it takes to make
a thing you keep. I know, because of him, intaglio printing means acid

etches a design into the plate. The artist marks through the soft ground
to create an image and the exposed areas become incisions to hold the ink.
Here then, in this print, nature's markings became incisions, became

the image. There's no clear metaphor for us in the print—we are both
artists. We were both the plate. Now, when I look at the image, I see
a thing the river made. I forget the artist. Moon after moon, I forgive.

On Me Such Legs Are Left

I wanted to drag

my father's family out

into the street   make them listen

to their decades of silence   make them

wrench their unmoved tongues from their mouths

the weight

the dregs of years

      I spent seeking

           their love and not my own

oh Lord   I return me to me

the letter *I* mine   not a steel beam but the cursive

lowercase one   like a contour of soft dirt

to sit down on   and the sun

Cento in Which I Lay the Line of My Body Next to the Women I Love to Address the Court of Men

The charcoal found its way from your hand
into the bones of daughters breaking—
sometimes the whole world of women
seems a landscape of red blood and things:
the color of daylight, cigarettes, ancient
bicycles, widows, motionless air. Desire
is a woman awake over a bowl of ashes.
I am no longer drunk on abstract theory
because I am hemmed in somewhere in
the basement of this life building. My art
practice is a high sunny window holding
me to the promise of release into the night.
Since you still do not know who I am,
I am inclined to brevity—you men crossed
my village with torches the night I was born
and I will address only the soft you, the you
that is me, the you that disavows the construction
of barriers. My great happiness is the sound
your voice makes calling to admit your despair.

Distant Mother

The AC window unit motors on. I feel the end of the world.
Skin blown bare from the low hum of the particle world.

Earthquake on the Oregon coast, a lopsided A-frame,
eventually the upper side plunges over the lower—water world.

Mother's hand pulls my 5-year-old chunk wrist across the street
to the neighbor's basement, a tornado etches away our world.

Not really telephone wire between us but static, blame
I heave onto her for not returning my calls. *It's a busy world.*

A counselor tells me being an adult-child is not the same
as a child-child—the beginning of my separate world.

I want her body to be like the letter *O*, different than
e in elegy, eucharist, flame—half circle bends to end the world.

I still long to hear her say *Katie Elizabeth*—my name
from her sharp smoker's mouth—a whole world.

Prayer for the Lover

Let me be the lover who delivers blood
      oranges in a blue cloth,

who hates sex for its joy costume of sound
      and loves sex as praise.

Let me be the lover who misses my mother
      and strings her freckles around my ears,

who lays heavy on the floor to count
      the valleys of my brother's chest,

who memorizes us undoing our wet clothes—
      a dare to swim naked in the moon.

Let what haunts me be sugar's history,
      not pleasure itself.

I trade a granule of sweet for a grain
      of sand. The sea. Let me

soak each feeling in bathwater
      and lap honey up with my tongue.

Let me circle my hips and break
        the glass lens I pin over us.

Let me crochet the sky into our skin
        and confess grief to the sun.

Notes

The opening epigraph by Louise Glück comes from "American Narcissism," found in her essay collection American Originality (Farrar, Straus and Giroux, 2017). Within the essay, a larger contextualization of Glück's notion of "that self" can be found. It became clear, later, that I had subconsciously constructed these poems around that greater notion.

"Father" was inspired by Allen Ginsberg's "Howl."

"Exaltation" was inspired by Alejandra Pizarnik's *A Musical Hell* (New Directions, translated by Yvette Siegert, 2013).

The epigraph by Lorna Dee Cervantes comes from "Shells" in her poetry collection *Emplumada* (University of Pittsburg Press, 1981).

"Excerpt from The Gold Club Trial: Mother" takes text directly from the broadcast, "CNN Transcripts, *The Point with Greta Van Susteren*: Were Some of the Country's Top Athletes Supplied With Sex at a Club Suspected of Having Mob Connections," aired on March 28, 2001.

"On Me Such Legs Are Left" is a line I rearranged from Gwendolyn Brooks' poem "my dreams, my works, must wait till after hell (*Selected Poems*, Harper & Row, 1963)" and the poem was inspired by *The Courage to Heal* by Ellen Bass and Laura Davis (Harper Perennial, 1994). The cento is made up of lines from Lorna Dee Cervantes, Gabriela Mistral, Louise Glück, Adrian Piper, Sor Juana Inés de la Cruz, Lucille Clifton, and Tracy K. Smith.

Gratitude

A warm thanks to the team at Alice James Books: Carey Salerno, Alyssa Neptune, Emily Marquis, Julia Bouwsma, and Debra Norton—what a pleasure. And to two of AJB's exquisite mentors: Lynn Melnick and Jill McDonough.

To the editors of the following journals in which versions of these poems first appeared: *Salamander, Redivider, Fence, Ruminate, Birdfeast, North American Review, Five Points, Cotton Xenomorph, The Rio Review,* and *Southern Indiana Review.*

To my teachers. Thank you for your time, patience, encouragement, and vision: Joy Castro, Kwame Dawes, Grace Bauer, Luis Othoniel Rosa, Ingrid Robyn, Hope Wabuke, Stacey Waite, Mark Wunderlich, Gregory Pardlo, Kathleen Graber, April Bernard, Major Jackson, Sven Birkerts, Megan Mayhew Bergman, and Joe Hoppe.

To my cohort at Bennington—what a dream to have been there with you. Jen Mathy: thank you for your immense and unwavering care. Lauren Conklin and Nathalie Elisabeth Boyle: you always have my heart sitting in the sun at Lake Paran.

To Russ Still and The Moonshiners: what sweet and unexpected support.

To those who read versions of this book in its many stages, nudged me toward more life-altering truths, were there when I got the call, and tolerated my obsessive fear of minor imperfections, I am forever grateful: Katie Schmid, David Henson, Ashley Strosnider, Paul Hanson Clark, Dwight Edward Brown III, Ángel García, David Winter, Jamaica Baldwin, Jordan Charlton, Jessica Poli, Teo Mungaray, Saddiq Dzukogi, Erika Luckert, Laura García García, Cecille Marcato, and Alexander Ramirez. If there are errors in my lines, gaps in my thinking—they are mine alone.

The biggest hug for Jamie! Thank you for making a refuge for me, many times. And then, for being like family. All my love to your people, who are my people: Parker, Isabella, Viva, and Sid.

I want to dedicate the labor it took to make this book to Tucker, Kai, and Mia. You are love itself and your life is your own. I am always here—you have every bit of my auntie heart.

To the dead. I honor your life. I heed your ghosts.

To my dearest friends. To Pecos.

And to my family, always. Love.

RECENT TITLES FROM ALICE JAMES BOOKS

Alice James Books is committed to publishing books that matter. The press was founded in 1973 in Boston, Massachusetts as a cooperative, wherein authors performed the day-to-day undertakings of the press. This element remains present today, as authors who publish with the press are invited to collaborate closely in the publication process of their work. AJB remains committed to its founders' original feminist mission, while expanding upon the scope to include all voices and poets who might otherwise go unheard. In keeping with its efforts to build equity and increase inclusivity in publishing and the literary arts, AJB seeks out poets whose writing possesses the range, depth, and ability to cultivate empathy in our world and to dynamically push against silence. The press was named for Alice James, sister to William and Henry, whose extraordinary gift for writing went unrecognized during her lifetime.

Designed by Pamela A. Consolazio

Spark
design

Printed by McNaughton & Gunn